WATER RESOURCES

WATER RESOURCES

TRUDY J. HANMER

FRANKLIN WATTS
NEW YORK | LONDON | TORONTO | SYDNEY | 1985
A FIRST BOOK

Diagram by Vantage Art, Inc.

Photographs courtesy of:
UPI/Bettmann, Inc.: opposite p. 1, pp. 16, 26, 44, 48,
51; Roger J. Cheng/State University of New York at
Albany: p. 7; AP/Wide World: p. 8; USDA-Soil Con-
servation Service: pp. 15, 29, 36; U.S. Navy: p. 19;
Bureau of Land Management, USDI: p. 23; U.S. Army
Corps of Engineers: p. 24; International Paper Com-
pany: p. 39; EPA/Steve Delaney: p. 41.

Library of Congress Cataloging in Publication Data

Hanmer, Trudy J.
Water resources.

(A First book)
Includes index.
Summary: Describes the nature of water, its sources
and cycles, and the problems of pollution and the
dwindling water supply.
1. Water. [1. Water] I. Title.
GB661.2.H36 1985   553.7   84-20857
ISBN 0-531-04919-1

CONTENTS

FOR KATE

INTRODUCTION

Water. We expect it to be there when we need it—to drink, to wash the car, to sprinkle the lawn, to boil an egg, to take a bath, to clean our clothes and dishes, to fill our fishbowls and swimming pools, to make lemonade and hot chocolate, to give the dog a bath—for thousands of uses every day. Most of us in the United States take water for granted. We assume that clean water will always be available.

But what do we really know about water? What is it? Where does it come from? Who pays for water? What does it cost? Will there always be enough?

We have always known the importance of water. It is basic to our existence. In prehistoric times people lived in caves located near a source of fresh water. The ancient Greeks believed that Oceanus, the god of water, was one of the two parents of creation. A Roman god, Aquarius, was believed to be the cupbearer to the other gods and the waterbearer to human beings. Ecclesiastes, one of the best-known books of the Bible, tells us that

"All the rivers run into the sea," and the Koran teaches, "By water, everything lives."

Scientists have known for centuries that water is necessary to sustain life. Aristotle, an early Greek philosopher and scientist, believed that the basic elements of the world were fire, earth, air, and water. Sir Isaac Newton, the seventeenth-century English scientist who made many important discoveries about the nature of gravity, believed that all human, animal, and plant life consisted mostly of water. It should not surprise us that when Helen Keller, blind and deaf, broke the dark wall of silence that imprisoned her, her first word was "water."

Water is not only all around us, it is also within us. Seventy-two percent of the earth's surface is covered by water, and 70 percent of the human body is composed of water. Our blood is 83 percent water, and our bones are 25 percent water. Water, which makes up most of our body fluids, helps us digest our food, cleanse our bodies of waste products, and carry nutrients, hormones, and disease-fighting cells to different parts of our bodies. We each need five to six glasses of water daily just to sustain these bodily functions. Some of this water is contained in the food we eat. For example, the apples we eat are 85 percent water, soft drinks are 90 percent water, hamburgers are 61 percent water, and peanut butter is 2 percent water. (That's why we get so thirsty when we eat a peanut-butter sandwich.)

We see water in many forms every day—as rivers, lakes, streams, and puddles. We see it in rain, snow, ice, and steam. We see clear water in our sinks and bathtubs and toilets, and we see dirty water running down the street into grates and off our buildings through gutters. Altogether there is a total of 369 quintillion, 820 quadrillion, 250 trillion gallons of water on earth. Most of us would have trouble imagining even one million gallons of water. Quintillions and quadrillions seem almost too large to think about. With so much water around, it is sometimes hard to understand why we worry about water shortages and why some people are never sure when they turn on their faucets that fresh, drinkable water will flow out. The fact is that most of the vast amount of water on earth—97 percent to be exact—is salty ocean water, which cannot be used for drinking or farming.

Over four trillion gallons of water fall on the continental United States every day in the form of snow, rain, sleet, or some other kind of precipitation. Yet there are people in the United States who cannot depend on a reliable supply of clean water whenever they need it because there is not enough rainfall or because the water has become polluted.

Water is so common in most Americans' lives that we do not really think about it much. We sometimes marvel at a spectacular waterfall or a major rainstorm, but plain everyday water is something we take for granted without knowing too much about it. In the next few years, Americans will have to change this way of thinking. Although the amount of water on earth has not changed since the beginning of time, the amount of clean water has. We are going to have to learn new ways to use our water so that we will always have clean water available to us.

We cannot live without water. It is important that we understand as much as we can about a substance that is so necessary to our lives.

CHAPTER ONE

THE NATURE OF WATER

What is water?

There are many ways to answer that question, but a chemist would reply this way: Water is a simple chemical compound. If you are not a chemist, that answer is still mysterious. You may wonder what a chemical compound is.

A chemical compound is formed when two or more elements join together. In the case of water, the two elements are hydrogen and oxygen. Many people who know very little about chemistry refer to water as H_2O. When they do that they are using water's chemical name.

Elements are made up of tiny atoms so small that they are impossible for the human eye to see. A group of atoms is called a molecule. In every molecule of water there are two hydrogen atoms, represented by the letter H and the number 2, which is always written below the line. There is also one oxygen atom, represented in water's chemical name by the letter O.

Each atom has a center called a nucleus, which contains protons and neutrons. Electrons are other parts of the atom; they circle the nucleus just as the planets circle the sun. When two hydrogen atoms and one oxygen atom join together to make a molecule of water, their atoms are attracted to each other and share electrons. Because of this attraction, the hydrogen and oxygen atoms stay together and form a water molecule, H_2O.

Knowing the chemical makeup of water is very important in understanding how water behaves. One of the reasons water is so valuable to us is that it acts in very special ways, different from the ways that almost all other chemical compounds behave. In spite of the fact that water is the most common liquid found on earth, scientists have still not discovered the key to all of water's secrets. We know how water acts, but we do not always know why.

We know that water can exist in three forms: as a liquid, as a solid, and as a gas. When it is a solid, we call it ice, and when it is a gas, we call it steam. Many other substances can be frozen solid or heated until they evaporate (turn into a gas), but only water does this regularly and at temperatures that are not extreme. On a cold day in Minnesota it is normal to see water frozen as ice on the streets. On a warm day in Florida it is just as normal to see water disappear from the hood of a newly washed car. The water has not really disappeared; it has evaporated as steam into the atmosphere. To make other substances freeze or evaporate, it may be necessary to be in a laboratory where temperatures can be lowered and raised far beyond what the human body can stand. Only water passes through the three stages of liquid, solid, and gas within a range of temperatures that can sustain human life.

When water freezes, it freezes from the top down. This happens because water is the only liquid that becomes less dense when it freezes. The reaction between the hydrogen and oxygen atoms makes water less dense as a solid than it is as a liquid. If ice became denser than water when it froze, the ice would sink to the bottom of a body of water where it could not be melted by the sun's warming rays. After a time all the water on earth would become frozen solid from the bottom up. If this happened, life on earth would not be possible.

Depending on the temperature and the time it takes to freeze, water makes different kinds of ice. So far scientists have discovered nine kinds of ice that can be distinguished from each other.

The two hydrogen atoms in the water molecule have a very special attraction for each other, and their chemical connection also greatly affects the way water acts. The bonding (a chemical term for the attraction between atoms) of the hydrogen atoms affects water's melting and boiling points, its *viscosity* (a measure of how quickly water pours; believe it or not, warm water pours faster than cold water), and its ability to dissolve other materials within it.

Scientists have found that almost all chemical substances can be dissolved in water. Because water is the only compound that has the ability to dissolve almost all other chemicals, it is very valuable to the chemical industry. At the same time this ability of water causes one of our biggest modern problems—water pollution. Because chemicals dissolve so easily in water, water has been called the universal solvent.

Another important chemical property of water is its stability. Many chemical compounds can easily be broken down into their basic elements by heating. This is not so in the case of water. When water is heated to a temperature as high as 4900°F (2700°C), only a very small part of the water breaks down into its two basic elements, hydrogen and oxygen. Because water is so stable, it is used as the basis for many scientific experiments.

In this highly magnified photograph of ice crystals, the many different patterns of ice can be seen.

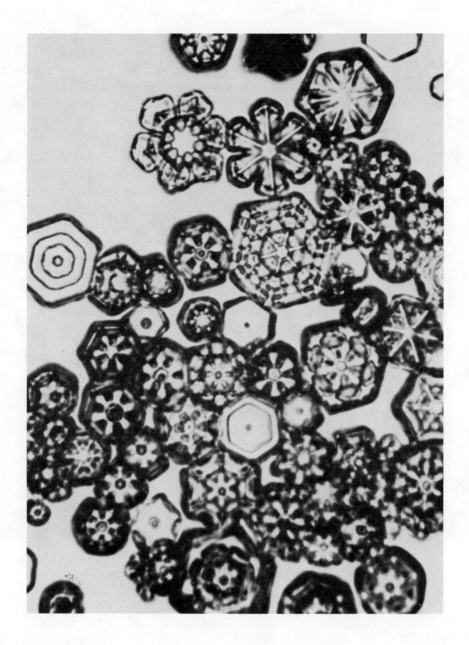

*Water has very strong surface tension,
as evidenced in this photograph
of raindrops on an automobile bumper.*

Scientists know that the water molecule will not break down into hydrogen and oxygen atoms in chemical reactions. Because the water molecule is so stable, chemical reactions of substances dissolved in water will not be affected by the atoms in water.

The chemistry of water also accounts for its very strong *surface tension*. Surface tension is a property of water (and other liquids) caused by the attraction of water molecules to each other. On the surface of the water, the molecules are even more strongly attracted to one another, forming a type of "skin." You cannot see this skin, but it is there. The skin tends to resist objects sinking into the water, which is why some bugs can walk on water. It also pulls water into drops. Surface tension in water is like the rubber in a balloon. The skin of the balloon pulls the balloon into a round shape, just as surface tension pulls water into a bead on a waxed car. Because of its surface tension, water clings to other things. One of the things water clings to is soil, and that is how water is able to enter the roots of growing crops to help them develop.

In the twentieth century scientists have discovered that they can alter the nature of water in such a way as to exaggerate the qualities that make water special. For example, firefighters can make water even wetter than it is—and more effective in fighting fires—by adding chemicals to it. In 1934 a scientist discovered *heavy water*, in which the hydrogen atom is heavier than a regular hydrogen atom. Heavy water, which scientists symbolize as D_2O (the D stands for *deuterium*), is composed of one atom of oxygen and two of deuterium. Heavy water has a different melting point and a different boiling point from that of ordinary water. Because of its special composition, heavy water is especially useful to scientists in the production of nuclear reactions, serving as a shield against stray, harmful atomic radiation.

Not only scientists, however, use the chemical properties of water. The earth itself could not exist without the continual chemical reactions that take place in nature every day. Within our bodies chemical reactions that involve water take place when we digest food and when we breathe. Human babies grow inside a water sac that protects them. Without that water they might be injured before birth. From eyelashes to toenails to lungs and stomachs, everything depends on water for its development. Over 85 percent of the earth's creatures are born, live their entire lives, and die in water.

CHAPTER TWO

THE WATER CYCLE

Where does water come from?

We know that there is a lot of water all around us. And we know that water falls from the sky in the form of rain and snow and sleet. Why doesn't the rain flood the earth? Where does the water go? Where do the rain and the snow come from?

The people who can answer all these questions are special scientists known as hydrologists. *Hydrology* means the study of water, and hydrologists are scientists who study water. In the Middle Ages people did not have a scientific knowledge of water. They believed that all water flowed from the center of the earth. Then in the 1600s, the British scientist Edmund Halley added up all the gallons of water in the rivers that flow into the Mediterranean Sea. He found that the total amount of water equaled the number of gallons of water that fell as precipitation on the areas drained by the rivers. He concluded that the amount of water that evaporates from the earth and that falls to the earth as precipitation is a constant. That means that the amount of water on the earth and within the earth's atmosphere never changes.

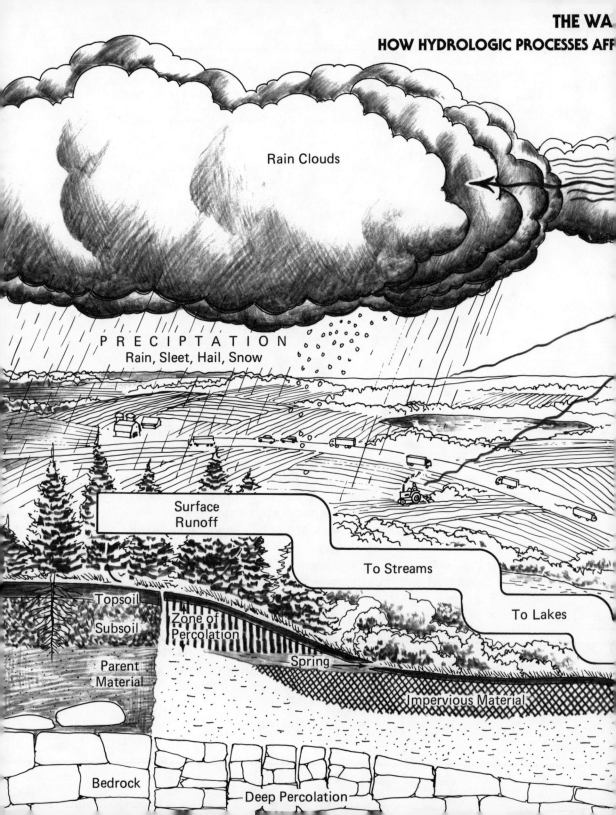

Rain Clouds

P R E C I P I T A T I O N
Rain, Sleet, Hail, Snow

Surface
Runoff

To Streams

To Lakes

Topsoil

Subsoil

Zone of
Percolation

Spring

Parent
Material

Impervious Material

Bedrock

Deep Percolation

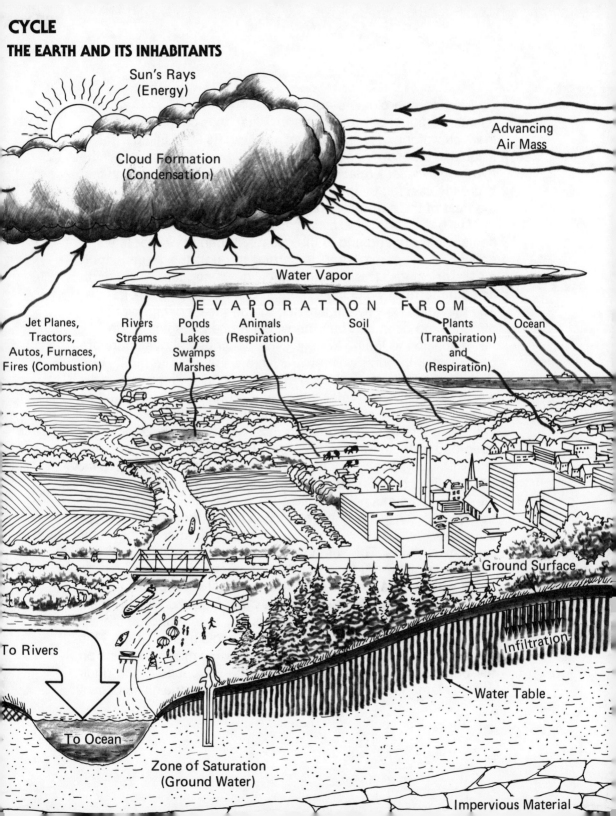

CYCLE
THE EARTH AND ITS INHABITANTS

Sun's Rays
(Energy)

Cloud Formation
(Condensation)

Advancing
Air Mass

Water Vapor

E V A P O R A T I O N   F R O M

Jet Planes,
Tractors,
Autos, Furnaces,
Fires (Combustion)

Rivers
Streams

Ponds
Lakes
Swamps
Marshes

Animals
(Respiration)

Soil

Plants
(Transpiration)
and
(Respiration)

Ocean

Ground Surface

Infiltration

To Rivers

Water Table

To Ocean

Zone of Saturation
(Ground Water)

Impervious Material

Modern hydrologists agree with Edmund Halley. There is a constant amount of water on earth. What does change is the form in which water exists. Water continually shifts from being a gas to a liquid to a solid. These changes are all part of what we call the *hydrologic cycle*, a relationship between water and the earth that is greatly affected by the pull of gravity from within the earth and the heat of the sun from outside the earth.

The basic hydrologic cycle can be described like this: The sun heats water on land and in the oceans. When the water is warm enough, it evaporates and is carried through the air as vapor, steam, or clouds. This moisture cools down and falls to the earth as some form of precipitation, most commonly as rain or snow. The rain and snow (when it melts) run off the land into rivers and streams and oceans. Then the whole process begins again.

In addition to the hydrologic cycle described above, there are other cycles through which water enters the air. The most common of these is *transpiration*. Transpiration is the process by which plants give up water to the air through their leaves, just as people give up moisture to the air through breathing and perspiring. When this water vapor cools, it falls onto the plants again, is absorbed by them for their use, and is then passed again into the atmosphere through transpiration. An acre of corn gives up over 3,000 gallons (13,650 l) of water daily, and a large hardwood tree may give up as much as 40,000 gallons (182,000 l) a day through transpiration. Whether the water cycle is one that involves evaporation or transpiration, the result is the same. None of the water really disappears. The same amount of water is still there; it just appears in different forms at different times.

The higher the temperature, the more water vapor can be carried by the air. That is why we can say that a hot August day feels muggy. What we are really sensing is the water vapor in the air. As the temperature drops, the moist air cools and rain falls. This same principle can be seen on a hot day when moisture forms on the outside of a glass of lemonade. The ice cubes in the drink cool the lemonade, which cools the glass; when the glass comes

An acre of corn gives up over
3,000 gallons (13,650 l) of water
daily through transpiration.

Surface water, such as this lake
in Tennessee, is the most abundant
type of water on earth.

into contact with the warm air, the water vapor cools and condenses as drops on the outside of the glass. This is what happens on a larger scale when it rains. On the average, 30 inches (76 cm) of rain fall on the continental United States annually.

After precipitation falls to earth in the form of rain or snow, it becomes either *groundwater* or *surface water*. Surface water is the water we can see—streams and rivers and lakes are all examples of surface water. When water falls onto the ground, most of it is absorbed into the soil, but it is not absorbed all the way to the center of the earth. At a depth of a few feet to a few hundred feet, most water meets hard rocks that stop it from sinking any farther. This surface water is the most abundant type of water on earth. Two-thirds of all American cities depend on surface water for their supply.

About a quarter of the earth's freshwater supply is groundwater. Groundwater fills all the spaces between the grains of rock or soil below the land surface and forms a body of water that is similar to a body of surface water such as a lake, but it is underground. The uppermost part of this body of groundwater is called the *water table*. Wells that intersect the groundwater can supply fresh water for drinking and farming. If the water table is close enough to the land surface, the groundwater can fill low spots or channels in the land surface. That is how most lakes and streams form.

Rock that contains a large amount of groundwater is called an *aquifer*. When a successful well is drilled, it is drilled in the area of one of these aquifers. One of the most interesting kinds of wells is a flowing *artesian well*. This is a natural well where the pressure of the rocks pushes the groundwater above the land surface so that the water seems to flow out of the ground. What people drilling any well always hope is that water from precipitation will refill the aquifer at the same rate that the people using the groundwater remove it from the aquifer. Although it is true that the total amount of water never changes, the amount of water in any particular aquifer can be used up if the water being taken is not returned at the same rate. For example, we will learn in chapter four of the problems with the Ogallala Aquifer, a huge groundwater reservoir in the western United States that has filled up over many thousands of years. Throughout the twentieth century, residents of many western states have been pumping water out of this aquifer at a rate far faster than the small amount of rainfall can replace.

The deeper the aquifer, the more expensive it is for people to get water from it. Wells must be dug deeper, and the pumps needed to bring the water to the surface are more costly to operate. The farther the pumps must carry the water, the more fuel is needed and the more expensive the operation. So, although people have long believed that water from aquifers is the purest water, it is less expensive for communities to get their water from surface sources such as rivers and lakes.

Abundant as surface water is, however, only a very small part of it is fresh water. Rainfall or the runoff from storms carries sediment from the land surface into streams and rivers and lakes. This sediment is different for different bodies of water, but the most common forms of sediment are quartz, gravel, sand, silt, and clay. Some sediment contains calcium and magnesium salts. These combine with soap in water to form insoluble matter that is difficult to rinse out of clothing. For that reason you may hear people speak of the difficulty of washing with "hard water." By that term they mean water that contains significant amounts of calcium and magnesium.

Other chemical compounds may be good in small amounts but harmful in larger amounts. Salt, a compound of sodium and chloride, is commonly found in surface water, sometimes in harmful amounts. The percentage of salt in water must be carefully watched by cities that use and reuse surface water supplies. Most water-quality specialists have determined that there should be no more than ¼ teaspoon (1.2 ml) of salt for every gallon (3.79 l) of drinking water. When there is too much salt in water used to irrigate plants, sodium from the salt causes the soil to form

U.S. Navy ships push together to move an iceberg blocking the channel at McMurdo Station, Antarctica. Icebergs are a potential source of fresh water.

clumps. Boron, an element that is also found in many surface water supplies, is good for people and plants in small amounts, but very harmful in large amounts. Many cities add fluoride to their water as protection against tooth decay. In small amounts this has proved to be a good practice, but too much of this same chemical can cause spots on tooth enamel.

Ice is a special kind of surface water. Some ice is permanent and never melts. This permanent ice, about 90 percent of which is found on the continent of Antarctica, rarely contains harmful chemicals and is thus a type of surface water that is a potential source of fresh water. (You will read more about this in chapter six.) In Antarctica scientists have found 5 million square miles (13 million sq km) of ice, often as much as 3 miles (4.8 km) thick. Only the topmost layer of this ice ever evaporates into the earth's atmosphere. The rest of this potential water supply is trapped as ice, seemingly forever, because of the extreme cold in this region.

Wherever we see water falling as rain or snow, flowing in rivers or lakes, or resting as ice in glaciers, we should recognize that in whatever form it appears, it is all part of the total amount of water available on earth. At various times water will change form as it goes through the stages of the hydrologic cycle. The water itself remains constant in both amount and chemical composition, but what is added to the water as it comes into contact with other substances both above and below the earth's surface is very important in determining how much fresh water is available for human use.

CHAPTER THREE

OUR WATER SOURCES

Where does the water come from when we turn on the faucet?

We have learned that the earth has an abundance of water—in rivers, lakes, oceans, and underground deposits. But this water is not necessarily clean and ready to drink. The muddy water that runs down the street after a rainstorm looks very different from the water we use to drink and bathe. Yet water from storms, called *runoff*, is one of the sources of the water we use in our homes. How does it get there, and how is it cleaned?

First, it is important to remember that although the amount of water in the world remains constant, water is distributed very unevenly. This means that some countries have much greater supplies of water than others. Even in the United States, some parts of the country have much larger water supplies than others.

Only one percent of all the water in the world is fresh water suitable for daily human use. This seems like a very small amount, but it is not. Some hydrologists have estimated that the freshwater supply available to the world is ten times what we need. Other scientists have calculated that in the United States alone there are over 6,000 gallons (27,300 l) of fresh water available for each person every day.

If all of this is true, why are people worried about water shortages? The answer has to do with water distribution. In those areas where people have very little water or have water of poor quality, the amount of clean water available to them is determined by technology. Whether it is in the form of pumps, reservoirs, windmills, dams, sewers, or water-purification plants, technology costs money.

We may think of water as being free or, at the most, very inexpensive. This has often been true in the past for people living in the United States, but as the procedures for obtaining *potable* (drinkable) water become more complicated, the cost of providing it becomes much greater. Having as much drinking water as we need—even more than we need—has been taken for granted by many Americans. This may not be true in the future.

If we look back at the patterns of settlement of the early American pioneers, we notice that they settled near bodies of water. As these settlements grew into towns and cities, it became necessary for local government officials to oversee the use of the local water supply. Eastern cities are among the oldest in the United States. In places like Boston, New York, Philadelphia, and Baltimore, city water systems that were constructed during the nineteenth century are still used today. Typically, these municipal systems carry water through miles of underground cast-iron pipes. These pipes (called street mains) are usually 4 to 6 inches (10 to 15 cm) in diameter and less than an inch (2.54 cm) in diameter when they enter houses and factories. Boston's city pipes were first laid in the 1840s. They are 1,100 miles (1,771 km) long and very expensive to repair. Although the city would like to have more modern pipes, Boston can afford to fix only one percent of these pipes each year.

New York City has a similar problem. North of the city abundant quantities of water are captured in *reservoirs* (large holding

The reservoir on the Deschutes River below Madras, Oregon, supplies water to nearby towns.

*This nineteenth-century aqueduct
supplies water to Washington, D.C.*

pools) and are then transported to the 800,000 buildings in New York City at the rate of 1.5 billion gallons (6.8 billion l) of water per day. The water is carried through two big tunnels, one of which was built in 1912 and one that dates from 1936. New York City water officials are worried that the tunnels may break down because they are now carrying much more water than they were designed to carry. A new tunnel is under construction, but its progress has been slow and expensive, and it will be a race to see if it can be finished before there is a major breakdown in one of the older tunnels. Some of the city's water pipes are made of wood, which was cheaper than metal in the 1800s when New York installed them. Wooden pipes break quite easily and cause small floods in subways, basements, and streets. Slowly these wooden pipes are being replaced by iron pipes.

Over 75 percent of all American cities use groundwater sources to get some of their water. This water is usually pumped to the surface by electric pumps. Such water is likely to contain dissolved minerals that come from the rock materials where the groundwater is found. The water may also contain animal or chemical wastes (pollutants). Because of the presence of these substances in the water, cities operate water-treatment plants that use a variety of methods to clean the water. In some systems a chemical called *alum* is added to the water. Alum attracts harmful bacteria (germs); the bacteria cling to the alum and are then removed with it. If the bacteria were left in the water, we probably would not see them or taste them, but they could cause diseases.

Other water treatments include filtering through a bed of very fine sand or charcoal. The sand removes particles of waste and sediment. A special kind of charcoal, called activated charcoal, is used to absorb harmful chemicals from the water that the sand cannot filter out. Still other treatment plants use a process called *aeration.* In this system, water trickles through gravel. Although few bacteria are killed this way, aeration does improve the taste and color of the water.

This offshore pumping station takes in water from Lake Michigan for transporting to a central water filtration plant to furnish water for the city of Chicago.

For killing bacteria the most common and effective water treatment to date has been the injection of *chlorine* into the water supply. In swimming pools you can often smell a strong chemical odor. This smell is usually produced by chlorine or a chemical closely related to it. These chemicals are added to swimming pools in fairly large amounts in order to kill the germs that might get into the pool from the many people swimming there. You do not drink pool water, and if you accidentally swallow some, it tastes bad. Chlorine is also found in most of our drinking water. However, it is added in small amounts—enough to kill bacteria, but not enough to taste bad or smell funny or to hurt us when we drink the water.

Before the discovery of chlorine as a water cleaner, epidemics of diseases were spread through city water supplies. Diseases like typhoid fever rarely break out in the United States today, but in the early 1900s (chlorine was first used in 1913), thousands of people died from this disease alone. Although we can now control the germs in our water supply, there are many substances that we cannot filter out completely. Dissolved salts, detergents, and chemicals are the most common of these substances and are potentially the most harmful.

In some areas the water that people use in their homes for drinking, cooking, washing, and bathroom purposes is recycled. These people may drink and cook with water that they have bathed in or flushed down their toilets earlier in the week. This is neither dirty nor dangerous. Their water tastes the same as that used by the people in New York City, where the water is not recycled. The sewage water in the cities that use recycled water is sent to sewage-treatment plants where it is cleaned, filtered, and purified for reuse. Remember, water is never "lost." The same amount is always available. So if a city can afford the expensive sewage-treatment plants necessary to clean its water for reuse, then that city does not need to worry if it is not located near a large freshwater supply.

For cities that do not recycle their water, used water is a problem. Sewer systems carry away used water—bathwater, cooking water, and water from toilets. But where does this "old" water go? If the water goes into a river or the ocean, some of the waste products in it are oxidized. Oxidation is the chemical process by which the oxygen in the water combines with the animal, mineral, and vegetable wastes in the water and changes them to less harmful substances. Sometimes, however, the load of sewage is too great for the water to be able to oxidize all of the wastes, or there are substances in the water that cannot be oxidized. In those cases the rivers and lakes into which the sewage flows are said to become polluted. Because of this, many cities have tried to build sewage-treatment plants where the wastes are removed from used water before it enters lakes and rivers.

The same principle of sewage removal is used by people living outside cities. People who live on farms and in small towns often have their own septic systems. These are tanks buried deep in the ground that capture the used water from people's homes and partially clean it before it runs off into the ground. Although some homes share septic systems, most homes in a neighborhood have their own septic tanks.

The greatest user of water throughout the United States and the world is agriculture. Farmers account for more than 80 percent of the water that is used by Americans every day. They need large amounts to irrigate their crops, especially in the western states where rainfall is scarce. The water that they use is clean groundwater or surface water, the same kind that western home-owners use for drinking and bathing. When we use water for cooking or cleaning, the water runs into our sinks and can be easily captured, cleaned, and reused. Water that is used for irrigation, however, is either "lost" into the ground or is passed into the atmosphere by plants (transpiration). Plants need a lot of water. For example, during the course of their growing seasons, alfalfa uses up 35 inches (89 cm) of water; sugar beets, 30 inches (76 cm); cotton, 25 inches (64 cm); and potatoes, 20 inches (51 cm). This water is not lost forever, of course, because no water

*An Arizona farmer opens the sluice gate
to irrigate a field of young alfalfa.*

is. It will return as rain when the water vapor in the air cools. However, the rain may fall hundreds of miles from the place where the plants were irrigated.

By whatever method we get our water—from city reservoirs, from streams or lakes, from the ground, or from water treatment plants—the amount of fresh, clean water available to us on a daily basis depends on where we live and what kind of water is available in our area. The farther we live from a natural water supply, the more likely it will be that the cost of adequate fresh water will continue to increase. The amount of water available to people living in the United States is enough for all our needs, if we can afford to distribute it evenly.

By looking at an area's average rainfall, we can tell whether or not that area is likely to have large supplies of water. On an average, the United States gets 30 inches (76 cm) of rainfall each year, but east of the Mississippi River the average annual rainfall is 40 inches (102 cm), in the Pacific Northwest it is 80 inches (203 cm), and in Nevada the average is only 9 inches (23 cm). People in Nevada can expect their local water supplies to be much smaller than those of people in Washington State. But if they are willing to pay more for their water, people in Nevada may be able to pipe it to their homes and businesses from regions that have more than enough for their own uses.

CHAPTER FOUR

WATER
PROBLEMS:
SUPPLY

If the United States has such an abundant supply of water, why are scientists worried about water shortages?

In spite of the fact that the United States has a lot of rainfall, many scientists believe that people in many parts of the country will face a critical shortage of fresh, clean water by the end of the twentieth century. This problem will result from the uneven distribution of water throughout the United States and is closely tied to a number of other issues, including questions about government regulation. Any discussion of water highlights the differences between farmers and city dwellers, agriculture and industry, public and private ownership of water utilities, and even western landowners and American Indians. Most of all, however, the talk of water shortages focuses on the wastefulness that has become an American habit.

In 1980 Americans used about 29 billion gallons (132 billion) of water per day, which averaged out to about 190 gallons (865 l) per person per day. Since 1900 the population of the United States has tripled, but American water use has increased well over six times. This means that we are using fresh water at a much faster rate than ever before. The increase has been especially sharp in the decades since World War II. For example, between 1970 and 1980 there was an almost 25 percent increase in water use per person per day. Even so, there is still more than enough water for everyone—potentially 7,500 gallons (34,125 l) per person per day. Distributing the supply evenly, however, has become more and more of a problem.

One of the biggest problems with our water supply is the amount of water that Americans waste every day. When our ancestors came to this continent, they believed that they had found a land of plenty. It seemed as though North America had more natural resources, including water, than could ever be used up. Early settlers wasted soil, forests, and water with little thought for the future. They believed that this land was so big that there would always be more. The wasteful habits and attitudes that they developed are still with us today. Each American uses up to 80 gallons (364 l) of water every day for private uses—3 or more gallons (14 l) to flush a toilet, 30 to 40 gallons (137 to 182 l) to take a bath, 20 to 30 gallons (91 to 137 l) to take a shower, 10 gallons (26 l) to wash dishes, and 20 to 30 gallons to wash a load of clothes. For these kinds of daily activities, we use much more water than do people in other countries. For example, we use three times as much water for private needs as do the people of Japan.

The people in Japan and in many other countries, such as Germany, Sweden, England, and France, pay much more for their water than we do. The price of water is very closely tied to the amount of water that is wasted. Experiments in different cities have proved that people are more careful about using water if it costs them more money. Some cities meter their water, which means that water users are charged for the number of gallons of water that they use. Other cities charge flat rates; each household pays the same amount of money whether they use 20 gallons (91 l) or 120 gallons (546 l) of water each day. People in cities that charge flat rates have been found to use twice as much water as people in cities that meter water use exactly. Because people are less wasteful of water when they pay for each gallon that they use, water meters help to conserve water.

Another problem with American water rates is that people in areas with very little water sometimes pay lower rates than people in areas with bountiful supplies. Water rates tend to be determined by politics and tradition rather than by the amount of usage. Rates may also depend on how easily the water can be obtained. Also, the costs of treating or purifying the water and distributing it to the many users can affect the rates that people pay. For example, in El Paso, Texas, where water is very scarce, water costs only fifty-three cents per 1,000 gallons (4,550 l). In Philadelphia, an area comparatively rich in water resources, the cost is $1.78 per 1,000 gallons. This kind of pricing does not seem sensible to the hydrologists who are trying to plan for the future of the nation's water supplies. They know that in Tucson, Arizona, a very dry area, the daily water use per person dropped from 200 to 140 gallons (910 to 637 l) between 1977 and 1980, when the price of water in that city was raised significantly. Hydrologists and city planners believe that the best way to preserve water supplies is for people to be less wasteful. They also argue that the best way to help people cut down their water use is to raise water prices. Water rates throughout the United States today, even where they are highest, are far less expensive than those in other industrialized countries. The cheap price of water encourages Americans to believe that their supply of water is endless.

Some hydrologists have calculated that if every household in California saved 75 percent of the water they now use for their daily needs, the savings would equal only a very small cutback by farmers. What this statistic illustrates is that farmers use much more water than individual homeowners. As you read earlier, agriculture accounts for over 80 percent of the annual water use in the United States. Most of this agricultural water is used for irrigation, especially in the western United States. Irrigation has enabled farmers to turn desert lands into rich farmlands. One of the questions facing the United States in the future is whether or not we can continue to afford the large amounts of water necessary to make western farms productive.

Much of the water used in the West—in Texas, Oklahoma, New Mexico, Kansas, Colorado, Nebraska, Wyoming, and South Dakota—comes from a huge underground source of water, the Ogallala Aquifer. This aquifer underlies an area of 174,000 square miles (450,660 sq km) and may well be the largest aquifer in the western United States. Because precipitation in this area is so scarce and the amount of water used for irrigation is so great, the Ogallala Aquifer is not being replenished as quickly as it is being drained. This huge aquifer provides the water for the 170,000 wells that irrigate 143 million acres (57.2 million hectares) of western land. This land produces 15 percent of the nation's wheat, corn, sorghum, and cotton and 38 percent of the nation's livestock. To irrigate the land that supports this production, eight times as much water is drawn from the Ogallala Aquifer each year as is replaced by precipitation.

The water from the Ogallala is relatively inexpensive because the federal government has a history of encouraging agriculture in the West. Yet there are some people who feel that we do not need to irrigate desert farmlands, especially when American agriculture produces far more than we can possibly use. These people argue that to deplete water supplies in this way is both wasteful and dangerous because someday the Ogallala will be dry. It takes 300 gallons (112.9 l) of water to produce one loaf of bread and 4,000 gallons (1,484.8 l) of water to raise each pound of beef. For this reason some people contend that agriculture should be carried on as much as possible in areas of plentiful rainfall, and that the irrigated deserts of the West are a luxury we can no longer afford.

At the very least, the opponents of desert agriculture believe that the price of water used for irrigation should be raised. In some areas water for irrigation purposes costs only nine cents per 1,000 gallons (371.2 l) and in some places the price is even lower if more water is used. This kind of pricing does not provide any incentive for farmers to save water. Farmers estimate that as much as 50 percent of the water used for irrigation is wasted. Changes in the irrigation methods used in the western states could result in huge water savings.

Currently most farmers use field flooding to irrigate their crops. This means that water is poured all over the field, even in the rows between the plants where no water is needed. Two other types of irrigation could also be used. One is sprinkler irrigation. By using huge sprinklers that reach out over the rows of plants, farmers can insure that up to 70 percent of the water actually reaches the crops. An even more efficient method of irrigation is drip irrigation, where the water is actually dripped directly onto each plant. With the drip system, up to 90 percent of the water would actually reach the plants. Both of these methods call for the installation of very expensive irrigation machinery. As long as farmers can obtain inexpensive water, there is no incentive for them to spend large amounts of money on new irrigation methods.

However, the water supply in the West is dwindling. There will soon come a time when farmers will have to irrigate more efficiently or stop farming altogether. Agriculture must be encouraged to develop new irrigation methods. If water supplies in the West run dry, not only the farmers but city dwellers and businesses throughout the country will suffer. During the past two decades more and more people have moved to the southwestern states in a population shift known as the migration to the Sunbelt. If these people cannot have fresh water for their new homes and businesses, they will be forced to return to the crowded northeastern states.

Farmers in the West are beginning to work on solutions to their water problems. They have long been in the habit of planting mesquite trees and salt cedars to protect their fields from wind

*Huge sprinklers are used to
irrigate crops in Montana's farmland.*

and soil erosion. In Arizona these plants use more water annually than do all of that state's cities. Farmers there are working to develop new plants that use less water or that thrive on "dirty" water and would not use up freshwater supplies.

A final problem facing water users in the West is the question of water rights on the reservations set up for American Indians in the late nineteenth and early twentieth centuries. According to an agreement made in 1908 between the federal government and the Native Americans, people living on the reservations are entitled to as much water as is necessary to irrigate their lands. What this means to western farmers is that reservation farmers have first claim on the West's water supply. As that supply gets smaller, the nonreservation farmers will be the first to be unable to irrigate their lands. There are more than fifty court battles currently raging as western farmers fight with the residents of the reservations over the question of water rights.

Although the water-supply problem seems to be more critical in the western United States, there are places in the East that are also facing shortages. The people of Long Island have recently realized that they are removing water from their aquifer more rapidly than the water is being replaced. Because the aquifers are being depleted, new wells are being installed at greater depths and at greater costs. In Massachusetts there have been several recent shortages of fresh water. Massachusetts has plenty of rainfall, but it does not yet have the storage capacity in its reservoirs to capture all the water required for its citizens' daily needs.

Hydrologists estimate that throughout the United States we lose as much as 20 percent of our fresh water every year through leaky faucets. If a faucet leaks one drop per second, 4 gallons (18 l) of water are wasted each day. Leaky toilets can waste as much as a gallon of water each hour. City planners hope that as the price of water rises, people will value their precious supply of water more highly and will help preserve this natural resource.

CHAPTER FIVE

WATER PROBLEMS: POLLUTION

What is water pollution? How does it affect our freshwater supply?

Pollution is a major reason for the decreasing supply of fresh water in the United States. When city water systems were first built in the nineteenth century, bacteria were the biggest threat to clean water. Today a whole host of new substances threatens the cleanliness of our water. Most of these are chemicals, the majority of which have been invented in the last forty years. Although most of these chemicals have beneficial uses in industry and agriculture, their presence in our water, even in small amounts, may be deadly. One of the biggest challenges facing the United States today is how to insure that the water we drink is clean.

There is no such thing as "pure water" outside a laboratory. We learned in chapter one that one of the unique properties of water is its ability to dissolve almost any other substance. Because of this characteristic, water acquires impurities as soon as it touches rocks or people or the pavement. We may think of

At an Alabama paper mill an aerator whips
waste water to put back oxygen that
is lost during the manufacturing cycle.
When the water is released, it will meet
government environmental standards.

rain as being pure water, but rain touches smoke and dust and tree leaves as it falls through the air. We used to think that water in underground aquifers was pure, but that water, too, comes into contact with earth and rocks and any waste substances that seep into the ground.

Some of the chemicals dissolved in water are good. During the nineteenth century it was fashionable and considered to be healthy for people to drink the water from mineral springs. This water contained large doses of such chemicals as calcium and sulfur. It often tasted funny and smelled worse, but people drank it. They believed, correctly, that certain amounts of some chemicals were good for them.

Earlier in the twentieth century, as we found out in chapter three, scientists found that the addition of chlorine to drinking water helped kill bacteria that carried diseases like typhoid fever. Later, however, scientists found that chlorine could not kill viruses nor destroy pesticides or herbicides—all harmful substances that are often found in water. Even more alarming is a recent scientific discovery that chlorine may react with natural elements in water to form a group of chemicals known as trihalomethanes, commonly called THMs. These THMs can cause many kinds of cancer.

THMs are not the only *carcinogens* (cancer-producing agents) found in our water. Since World War II the petrochemical industry has grown tremendously in this country. Petrochemicals are substances produced by combining different chemicals usually found in natural oil and gas. The petrochemical industry has developed between 1,000 and 2,000 new compounds a year since 1970. These compounds have many very valuable uses in industrial production. Problems arise when industries have to

Leakage from petrochemical dump sites is a threat to our water supplies.

dispose of the waste by-products that are produced when petrochemicals are used. A common method of disposal has been to dump them underground. There are over 50,000 such dump sites in the United States today. What we are just beginning to realize is that leakage from these dump sites has meant that very harmful chemicals have seeped into our water supplies.

The United States Environmental Protection Agency (EPA), a government organization responsible for protecting our natural resources, has estimated that about one-half of the water supply in the United States faces contamination from petrochemicals. To deal with this and other water pollution problems, Congress passed a Water Pollution Control Act in 1972 and a Safe Drinking Water Act in 1974. Both acts were designed to provide federal funds to help clean up our water. The problem is a huge one, not only throughout the United States but in most of the industrialized nations of the world as well.

Perhaps the most widely publicized example of petrochemical water pollution occurred at the Love Canal in Niagara Falls, New York. A chemical plant in this area had buried more than twenty million pounds (9.07 million kg) of chemical wastes in an old canal once intended for use as a barge canal. The wastes had seeped through the ground to the land surface and were a danger to people and pets in the area. When the problem was identified and the leaking chemicals were tested, they were found to contain dangerously high levels of carcinogens. Families who had lived by the canal for years were forced to give up their homes and move.

Although the Love Canal situation is a dramatic example of underground chemical pollution, it is far from being the only one. Other areas of the country have had their water supplies contaminated by another carcinogen, trichloroethylene (TCE). TCE is a commonly used grease-cutting chemical. In western Pennsylvania and in the San Gabriel Valley of California, wells have had to be closed down when TCE was found in the water. As at the Love

Canal, the chemical had seeped through the ground from an industrial dump site to the water supply.

In the cases of the Love Canal and the San Gabriel Valley, the sources of the pollution could be identified. More troublesome is "nonpoint source" pollution, which means chemical contamination of the water supply that cannot be traced to any specific source. This means that harmful chemicals can creep underground for miles, but it is difficult to predict where these chemicals will emerge or where they come from. Scientists estimate that millions of people in poor rural communities have water that has been contaminated by wastes from a variety of industries, but it is impossible to determine the exact sources of this pollution. In 1969 the surface of the Cuyahoga River near Cleveland, Ohio, caught fire and burned for eight days. Since water does not burn, it was obviously the flammable chemical pollutants in the water that were burning. These substances came from many of the Cleveland-area industries, not just one or two. Again in Ohio, in 1979 the EPA found 700 synthetic chemicals in Cincinnati's drinking water. Chemical pollution is also responsible for the condition we call "acid rain." Water vapor passing over the industrial cities of the Midwest picks up harmful chemicals that fall in rain over the Adirondack Mountains of New York. Acid rain is blamed for killing fish and other waterlife in that area.

Industrial waste is not the only source of chemical pollution. At Times Beach, Missouri, residents were horrified when spring floods washing over their property were found to contain very high levels of dioxin, one of the most toxic synthetic substances. The dioxin was part of waste oil that had been sprayed on roads in Missouri in the 1970s to keep the dust levels down. Milwaukee, Wisconsin, has also found that its roads are a source of pollution. Storm runoff from the paved surfaces of Milwaukee contains very high levels of lead, zinc, copper, and chromium. Ten percent of all the salt produced on earth is used by U.S. cities to melt ice on their streets. The salt is easily dissolved in storm runoff.

Seattle, Washington, has separate storage areas for storm runoff, where the water is collected and treated. Remedies like this one are expensive.

Nevertheless, it is even more expensive to clean up water after an area has been polluted than it is to prevent the pollution in the first place. To clean up the dioxin pollution in Times Beach, for example, will cost over $30 million. And the cost of pollution in dollars does not include the possible costs in human health.

Chemicals are not the only source of water pollution, however. Many cities do not have adequate sewage-treatment plants, and they are therefore forced to dump raw sewage (human waste, bathwater, cooking water) into lakes and rivers. New York City alone dumps over 200 million gallons (910 million l) of sewage a day into the East River and the Hudson River. The Potomac River near Washington, D.C., was once choked with algae that thrived on the sewage that was flushed into that body of water.

Recent efforts to clean up the Potomac, as well as a number of other cleanup programs throughout the United States, seem to have been successful. Improved water quality in Ohio's Cuyahoga River, Lake Erie, and the Androscoggin River in Maine are examples of successful antipollution campaigns. As new sources of pollution are identified, new methods of combating them must be found. The EPA has recently estimated that over eighty U.S. cities have water that contains carcinogenic chemicals. The solutions to this kind of problem are controversial. For example, the EPA believes that charcoal filters could be installed in household water supplies for a very small price. These charcoal filters could trap many of the cancer-producing chemicals and prevent them

*In New York State's Adirondack Mountains
a helicopter drops lime into a lake in an
effort to counter the effects of acid rain.*

from entering the drinking-water supplies. Many water companies disagree about both the cost and the effects of the charcoal filters. When problems are new and solutions have not yet been tested, there is bound to be a great deal of disagreement about how the problems can be solved. This is certainly true of the problems surrounding water pollution. However, everyone agrees that the problems exist and that solutions must be found.

CHAPTER SIX

THE OCEANS: A SOURCE OF FRESH WATER

Could the water in the oceans be one solution to our freshwater supply problems?

We know that 97 percent of all the water on earth is what we call salt water. This salt water can be found in the United States in inland lakes such as the Salton Sea and Mono Lake in California and the Great Salt Lake in Utah. Salt water is also found in rivers such as the Salt River in Arizona and in low-lying marshy areas near the coasts. But by far the greatest source of salt water for the United States or any other nation that borders on the sea is the ocean. Most of the enormous amount of salt water on earth is contained in its great oceans.

What do we mean when we call ocean water salt water? If you have been swimming in the ocean, you know that ocean water tastes salty and is sticky when it dries on your skin. The sticky feeling comes from the salt that is left behind when you dry off in the sun and the water on your body evaporates. As you learned in chapter one, water is a very good solvent. Because of this property, all kinds of mineral compounds—called salts—are eas-

ily absorbed into water. The most common salt found in sea water is ordinary table salt. However, many other types of salts are also present in the ocean. Most of these are combinations of such elements as calcium, magnesium, sodium, sulfur, carbon, chlorine, and oxygen. The chemical name for ordinary salt is sodium chloride ($NaCl$). This is the chemical compound that results when sodium and chlorine combine.

Almost all bodies of water have some salt in them. A mountain stream far away from the ocean may contain as few as fifty parts of salt for every million parts of water. The oceans average 35,000 ppm (this abbreviation means parts of salt for every million parts of water). This is another way of saying that the oceans are 3.5 percent salt. This is a very high percentage, which explains why you can taste the salt in ocean water but not in mountain streams. Sometimes river water becomes salty because of industrial pollution, or when irrigation water washes salts from the soil into rivers, or because the ocean mixes with river water near the coast by action of the tides, or because of heavy irrigation use of water that runs off the land into the river. When the water becomes so salty that it tastes too unpleasant to be used for drinking and cooking, we say that the water is brackish. People in western states are very concerned that their water is becoming brackish because of heavy irrigation use. In 1980 some parts of the Columbia River were found to have a salt content as high as 740 ppm, and the Rio Grande in Texas registered 754 ppm.

Scientists have long sought a way to purify brackish water and to convert ocean water to fresh water suitable for human uses. They have discovered many ways to do this, but most of

Ninety-seven percent of all the water on earth is salt water, most of which is found in our oceans.

the methods are too expensive for widespread use. Since 1952 the United States Department of the Interior has had a special branch of government called the Office of Saline Water. *Saline* is another word for salty, and discovering how to convert salt water to fresh water is one of the major responsibilities of the people working at the Office of Saline Water.

Removing the salt from sea water is called *desalinization, desalination,* or just *desalting.* The oldest method that people know about is also the easiest. This is the process called *distillation.* If water is heated, it turns to water vapor and leaves its salts behind. The water vapor is cooled to turn it back into liquid. This liquid is fresh water. If the goal is to produce small amounts of water, this is a very simple and efficient process to use. Many people distill water in their homes for use in their irons. The small amount of salt in ordinary drinking water, although not tasted by us, would cling to the inside of the steam iron and eventually clog the steam holes.

Distillation is very expensive if it is used on a larger scale. The amount of energy necessary to heat and then cool the water makes distillation of large amounts of water too costly. Because of these energy problems, scientists have invented a modified process called flash distillation. They reason that water evaporates more quickly if it is under pressure. So, they put large amounts of water under so much pressure that it changes very quickly—flashes—into water vapor when the pressure is suddenly released. The vapor is then cooled and condensed. Pressurizing the water costs money and uses energy, but not as much as heating water at normal pressure. Flash-distillation plants are in use in many communities and provide many people

This desalinization plant at Guantanamo Bay, Cuba, supplies water for the U.S. Naval Base located there.

with clean but expensive water. One of the largest flash-distillation plants is located in Key West, Florida, an island surrounded by the ocean.

Another similar process for desalting water is freeze distillation. Just as water vapor leaves salts behind, so does ice. This process is sometimes called *crystallization.* When water crystallizes—forms ice—the ice is composed of pure water. The ice can then be rinsed to remove any salts clinging to it, melted, and used for household purposes. The problem with this process is that it is as expensive to freeze water and then melt the ice as it is to heat the water and then cool the water vapor.

Because icebergs are formed by crystallization they contain no salt although they are frozen sea water. In fact, some Arab countries are studying the possibility of using tugboats to push giant icebergs from the Arctic Ocean to desert lands. The trip would take several months because the icebergs are so big, and a lot of water would melt on the journey to the warm climate. Enough ice would remain, however, to make the project worthwhile. It is estimated that a medium-size iceberg, 1,000 feet (305 m) long, 500 feet (152 m) wide, and 200 feet (61 m) high would hold about 750 million gallons (276.5 million l) of fresh water in the form of ice.

A third type of desalinization is the process of *reverse osmosis.* In this process the salts are squeezed out of the water. The water is screened through microscopic holes that are just large enough for the water molecules to pass through, but too small to allow the salt molecules to pass. In order for reverse osmosis to work, the water must be pushed against the screen by enormous pressure. Again, the costs are high because of the energy needed to push the water so hard against the screen.

Because of the chemical nature of both salt and water, scientists have been able to devise yet another method of desalinization. Salt dissolved in water does not exist as the compound NaCl, but instead exists as separate sodium and chloride ions. Ions are special atoms that carry a very small electric charge.

Electric charges make things cling to other things. For example, it is the static electricity in a clothes dryer that makes socks cling to sheets. Scientists have invented small electrical screens through which water can be passed. The salt ions cling to the screens, and the pure water flows through. This process is called *electrodialysis.* It has been used at a major desalination plant in Buckeye, Arizona, since 1962. Another desalting plant at Webster, South Dakota, also uses electrodialysis. In Webster, scientists continually experiment to perfect this electric process in order to make it more economical.

The newest form of distillation to desalinize ocean water also uses the least costly energy. This is the *solar still.* A solar still operates on energy from the sun—free energy—and acts almost like a greenhouse. A solar still is a basin with a glass cover. Water in a solar still evaporates because of the heat of the sun. The brine (the salty residue that is left behind when the water evaporates) runs out the bottom, the vapor is collected, allowed to condense (turn back into water) as the sun goes down, and then runs as fresh water from a tube connected to the still. Although energy costs for solar stills are very low, this method presents some major problems. A still with a glass cover 64 square feet (5.76 sq meter) produces only one gallon of fresh water per day, so stills have to be very, very large to produce usable amounts of water. The sun is free, but it does not always shine. Consequently, stills can only operate in areas where there is frequent, very hot sunshine. Also, solar stills can be expensive to build.

Desalination of sea water may be one of the answers to our water supply problems in the future. However, there are still many problems to be worked out. Chief among these is cost. The energy required for all of these methods (except solar distillation) makes desalinization very expensive. Where desalting plants are in operation in America—in Freeport, Texas; San Diego, California; Wrightsville Beach, North Carolina; and Roswell, New Mexico, for example—people pay very high prices for their water. At Coalinga, California, the site of the nation's first desalting plant, people fill jugs with water at a water pump in much the same way that people in other areas of the country fill their cars at gas pumps. But water is expensive for the people of Coalinga. It costs them two cents a gallon, which is ten cents every time they flush a toilet and sixty cents every time they take a shower. In the early 1980s the nationwide average price for water was fifteen cents per 100 gallons (455 l). For people whose water came from desalinization plants, the price was one dollar per hundred gallons.

In spite of high costs, desalinization is growing in popularity. In 1950 there was no desalting plant capable of producing even 20,000 gallons (91,000 l) of fresh water per day. By the end of the 1970s, desalting plants produced more than a billion gallons of fresh water per day, and there were many plans for new plants. However, even with this growth, and even if more efficient energy sources can be found, desalinization still faces difficulties. People living in Kansas and Colorado—without ready access to the oceans—will probably continue to rely on rivers and groundwater for their water supplies because transport of desalinized ocean water would be too expensive.

CHAPTER SEVEN

THE FUTURE

What can we do to preserve our water supplies?

The United Nations has named the 1980s the International Drinking Water Supply and Sanitation Decade. In this way the United Nations recognizes that the preservation of clean water is one of the biggest challenges facing the people of all nations in the foreseeable future.

Here in the United States we are gradually awakening to the water crisis that will threaten us if we do not take steps now to conserve our water supplies. It is not too late. As Mark Twain, one of America's most famous authors, once wrote, "When the well's dry, we know the worth of water." For the first time in American history, it looks as though the well could run dry; unlimited supplies of inexpensive, clean water are no longer available. As our national water supply begins to dwindle, we realize more than ever how much water means to us. Water is our most precious resource, but many of us continue to waste water with seemingly little regard for the future. Just as petroleum shortages created a resource crisis in the 1970s, water shortages could develop into the resource crisis of the 1980s.

And yet we know that we have plenty of water in the United States. On Mount Waialele Kauai in Hawaii, 624 inches (16 m) of rainfall is recorded each year. At Silver Springs, Florida, the area that Ponce de Leon, a Spanish explorer, sought as the Fountain of Youth, 800 million gallons (303 million l) of fresh water pour out of the ground as springs and streams each day. As we have learned, the question is one of uneven distribution. Most Americans do not live in Hawaii or in Florida. There are some states, like California and Colorado, where the people live mainly in one part of the state, but most of the water is located in other parts. In California 60 percent of the rainfall occurs in the north, but two-thirds of the water use occurs in the south. In Colorado 80 percent of the people live east of the Rockies, but 70 percent of the water is located west of the Rockies.

The question is not solely one of uneven distribution, however. Some parts of the country have always had more water than other parts of the country. What is new is the depletion of water supplies in parts of the country that thought they had enough underground water to use forever—places like Long Island, in New York State, Florida, and Western cities above the Ogallala Aquifer. In these places people must learn to change old and wasteful habits and find new ways of using dwindling supplies of water more efficiently. Today Arizona farmers are paying far higher prices for water than they used to. This is Arizona's attempt to force its citizens to use more efficient irrigation systems.

Throughout the country homeowners are installing new toilets that require only half as many gallons of water for flushing as older models. People are using new shower heads that restrict the flow of water each time someone takes a shower. Each of these small steps helps, but the biggest conservation must be undertaken by the largest water users. Cities must prepare to spend lots of money to improve leaky water systems and to develop less costly ways of treating water for human use. They must investigate the construction of new systems that will provide one set of pipes for pure drinking and cooking water and another set for less pure water that could be used for such purposes as washing cars and sprinkling lawns. All the people who use water will have to help pay for these projects through higher water prices.

Finally, we must all look for new ways to control water pollution. Money must be spent to clean up waste dumps before harmful chemicals sink into the ground. Industries must be forced to choose new dump sites carefully so that groundwater will not be contaminated, and those sites must be inspected regularly to insure that leakage of the chemicals does not occur. Since 1972 the federal government has spent $37 billion and American industry has spent $16 billion just to control sewage. As with new conservation methods, money from everybody's water bill must go toward the fight against pollution.

To conserve and protect our water supplies will be expensive. There is no better way for us to spend money. Without water, there can be no life.

GLOSSARY

aeration—a water-cleaning process in which the water is trickled through gravel.

alum—a chemical which is used to remove harmful bacteria from water.

aquifer—a rock containing a large amount of groundwater.

artesian well—a natural well in which the pressure of rocks pushes the groundwater above the land surface.

carcinogens—cancer-producing substances.

chlorine—an element used for water purification.

crystallization—a desalinization process in which water is frozen to remove impurities.

desalinization (desalination, desalting)—the process of removing salt from sea water.

distillation—the oldest method of desalinization; the process of heating water to separate the water vapor from any salts it may contain.

electrodialysis—the desalinization of water by an electric process.

groundwater—water that lies in pools beneath the ground.

heavy water—deuterium oxide, a special form of water in which the hydrogen atom is heavier than a regular hydrogen atom.

hydrologic cycle—the relationship between water and the earth caused by the pull of gravity and the heat of the sun.

hydrology—the study of water.

potable—drinkable.

reservoir—large holding pool.

reverse osmosis—a desalinization process in which impurities are squeezed out of the water.

runoff—water that runs along the surface of the ground after storms.

saline—salty.

solar still—a basin with a glass cover used in the desalinization of water by distillation from the heat of the sun.

surface tension—the property of water caused by the attraction of the water molecules to each other.

transpiration—the process by which plants give up water to the air through their leaves.

viscosity—the measure of how quickly water pours.

water table—the depth below which an area of the ground is completely filled with water.

INDEX